I0796106

Middle Eastern American WOMEN OF ACHIEVEMENT

Stephen Currie

San Diego, CA

Printed in the United States

For more information, contact:
ReferencePoint Press, Inc.
PO Box 27779
San Diego, CA 92198
www.ReferencePointPress.com

LIBRARY OF CONGRESS CATALOGING-IN-PUBLICATION DATA

Names: Currie, Stephen, 1960- author
Title: Middle Eastern American women of achievement / Stephen Currie.
Description: San Diego, CA : ReferencePoint Press, 2026. | Series: Women of achievement | Includes bibliographical references and index.
Identifiers: LCCN 2025003091 (print) | LCCN 2025003092 (ebook) | ISBN 9781678210625 library binding | ISBN 9781678210632 ebook
Subjects: LCSH: Arab American women--Biography--Juvenile literature | Hanna-Attisha, Mona--Juvenile literature | Kotb, Hoda, 1964---Juvenile literature | Slaiby, Rima Fakih--Juvenile literature | Almutairi, Adah, 1976---Juvenile literature | Tlaib, Rashida, 1976---Juvenile literature | LCGFT: Biographies
Classification: LCC E184.A65 C87 2026 (print) | LCC E184.A65 (ebook) | DDC 920.0092--dc23/eng/20250328
LC record available at https://lccn.loc.gov/2025003091
LC ebook record available at https://lccn.loc.gov/2025003092

CONTENTS

Middle Eastern American Women

Other than all being young American women, it may be difficult to imagine at first what race car driver Toni Breidinger, newly elected US representative Yassamin Ansari, and pop singer Elyanna have in common. The three have very different backgrounds, interests, and achievements. Breidinger is the one of the very few women competing on the NASCAR racing circuit. Ansari, upon taking office in January 2025, became one of the youngest members of the US House. Elyanna is a singer-songwriter who gained fame on Instagram and sold out her North American tour in 2024. It would be hard to imagine three public figures as different as these.

But Breidinger, Ansari, and Elyanna all share an important heritage: they all have roots in the countries of the Middle East. One branch of Breidinger's family comes from Lebanon, Ansari is of Iranian descent, and Elyanna and her family arrived in the United States from Palestine. All three take pride in their family backgrounds and see themselves as connected to their ancestral homelands as well as to the Middle East in general. "I feel like I have developed a very solid fan base of Arabs that like to come to races,"[1] says NASCAR's Breidinger. Ansari speaks proudly and enthusiastically of her family's connection to an Iranian cultural center in her hometown of Phoenix, Arizona. Similarly, Elyanna has often sung in Arabic in concert. "It was very exciting," she said about doing so at the 2023 Coachella Valley Music and Arts Festival, "and it's not only for me, it's for our culture, for our people."[2]

> "The arts need a fresh kind of fire, something that [Deana] Haggag embodies with passionate devotion and an approach that feels both thoughtful and innovative."[3]
>
> —Rebecca Bengal, journalist

Middle Eastern American women, today and in the past, have risen to distinction in every field of endeavor. Christa McAuliffe, the teacher-turned-astronaut who tragically died in a space shuttle explosion in 1986, could trace her mother's family to Lebanon. Both of White House press corps journalist Helen Thomas's parents were born in what is now Lebanon, while movie star Salma Hayek's father is Lebanese. Gigi Hadid is a supermodel of Palestinian descent. The father of Queen Naija, a vlogger, singer, and media personality, is from Yemen. Egypt-born Eman Ghoneim is a noted geomorphologist, a scientist who

Toni Breidinger is of Middle Eastern descent and also one of the very few women competing on the NASCAR racing circuit.

studies landforms and how they develop. Rana El Kaliouby, also an Egyptian immigrant, was a research scientist at the Massachusetts Institute of Technology and is now the chief executive officer of a science-based company. Deana Haggag, whose parents are Egyptian immigrants, is well known for her work in museums and arts administration. "The arts need a fresh kind of fire," journalist Rebecca Bengal writes approvingly, "something that Haggag embodies with passionate devotion and an approach that feels both thoughtful and innovative."[3]

Some of these women have overcome significant barriers stemming from sexism as well as prejudice related to their ethnicity or religion. Laura Nader, whose parents were Lebanese, was the first woman to receive tenure—which allows professors to remain at their institution throughout their career—in the anthropology department at the University of California, Berkeley, in the early 1960s. Politician Rashida Tlaib, among others, has spoken frequently about the prejudice she has faced as a Muslim American with roots in Palestine. Others have achieved despite personal hardships. In 1980, for example, Candace Lightner's daughter was killed by a drunk driver. In response, Lightner, whose mother's family were Syrian immigrants, founded an advocacy group called Mothers Against Drunk Driving. Similarly, Zainab Salbi grew up in a war zone in Iraq. She has since started an organization called Women for Women International, which works with women who have survived wars and helps them escape poverty and oppression.

Somewhere between 3.5 million and 4 million Americans have Middle Eastern heritage. That amounts to only a little over 1 percent of America's population, and half of this percentage consists of men and boys. But though there may be comparatively few American women of Middle Eastern heritage in the US population, these women have had an important impact. From business and politics to technology and the visual arts, from New York to California, American women of Middle Eastern heritage have worked to make their dreams come true, to pioneer within their fields, and in many cases, to improve the lives of others.

CHAPTER ONE

Mona Hanna, Pediatrician

American history is filled with the courageous actions of whistleblowers—people who alert the public to activities that are harmful or illegal. As long ago as 1906, for example, author Upton Sinclair exposed unsanitary practices in meatpacking plants in his book *The Jungle*. New York police officer Frank Serpico brought attention to widespread corruption in his department in the late 1960s. And in 1974 chemical technician Karen Silkwood testified about unsafe working conditions in the nuclear power plant where she was employed. Since whistleblowers are taking on powerful corporations, government entities, and institutions, they are subject to verbal attacks and physical harm. But they persevere regardless.

The tradition of whistleblowing continues in the twenty-first century. One of the best examples took place in 2015, when a Middle Eastern American physician, Mona Hanna-Attisha (now known as Mona Hanna), demonstrated that the municipal water in her city was unfit to drink. Like earlier whistleblowers, Hanna was battling powerful interests, in her case state and city governments. Despite efforts to discredit her and her research, Hanna continued her fight and eventually convinced her opponents that she was right. Hanna is known today for her efforts to tell the truth about the water—and for her courage in not giving up.

Dr. Hanna demonstrated that the municipal water in her city was unfit to drink. Despite efforts to discredit her, Hanna continued her fight and eventually convinced her opponents that she was right.

Early Years

Though Mona Hanna was born in the United Kingdom and grew up in the United States, her family's roots were in Baghdad, Iraq. Mona's father, David, was a metallurgist, a scientist who studies the behavior of metallic elements. Mona's mother, Talia, was also a scientist; during the early 1970s she was one of just two women studying advanced chemistry at Baghdad University. Around 1974 the couple moved with their son, Mark, to Sheffield, England, where David entered a doctoral program. Mona was born in Sheffield in 1976. The long-range plan was for the family to return to Baghdad after David had his degree. David would get a job in Iraq's nuclear industry, and Talia would work as a chemist.

Iraq, however, was a dangerous place to live during the 1970s. It was governed by a brutal dictatorship, and many young adults, especially highly trained professionals, were leaving the country for good. David recognized that a return to Iraq might require him to develop nuclear weapons for a deeply repressive government, one that spied on its citizens and used torture against its own people. While the Hannas hoped to return to their homeland, it seemed doubtful that conditions in Iraq would change soon. Accordingly, when the family left England, they did not go back to the Middle East. Instead, they headed to Houghton, Michigan, where David engaged in further metallurgical research.

Mona's family eventually settled in Royal Oak, Michigan, near Detroit. David worked as a researcher for a car manufacturer, and Talia taught English to fellow immigrants. "It wasn't the life they'd anticipated," Hanna told an interviewer years later, "but they quickly recognized that this was their home. They set their minds to making the best of it, and to raising their children to be grateful for the freedom and opportunities available to them."[4] Their methods were effective. Mona did well in elementary and high school and was elected senior class president. "It wasn't that she was the most popular kid, she was popular with every group," remembers Mark. "She was able to bring everybody together."[5]

> "It wasn't that she was the most popular kid, she was popular with every group. She was able to bring everybody together."[5]
>
> —Mark Hanna, Mona Hanna's brother

As a high school student, Hanna was concerned about the environment. She joined an ecological club at school, which organized recycling drives and put on plays about nature for elementary students ("I was always Mother Earth,"[6] she recalls). But the club also engaged in real-life activism, raising awareness about pollution in their community and campaigning to elect an environmentalist candidate to the state legislature. Following high school, Hanna went on to study environmental science and sustainability at the University of Michigan in nearby Ann Arbor.

But after college, Hanna decided to become a physician rather than pursuing a career in environmentalism. She obtained a medical degree from Michigan State University and a master's degree from the University of Michigan School of Public Health. Choosing a medical specialty was easy for her. "As a medical student, you have to do rotations in a variety of fields," Hanna wrote years later, "and as soon as I got to pediatrics, I knew I was at

The Immigrant Experience

Mona Hanna is a strong supporter of immigrants and immigration in general. In her 2018 book, *What the Eyes Don't See*, she shared the benefits her family experienced by leaving Iraq for the United States and contrasted her journey with the challenges faced by Flint's children.

> As it had for so many immigrants over the centuries, the promise of America worked for my family. We'd left a country that was broken, unsafe, unpredictable, and oppressing its own people for a country that allowed us to thrive. My parents didn't have much when they arrived in the United States, but they were able to use their educations to find good-paying jobs, buy a house in a safe neighborhood, and educate Mark and me at Michigan's excellent public schools and universities. The American Dream—buoyed, backed, and underwritten by the choices of the American people, expressed through their democratically elected government—worked for us in so many ways that it no longer works for my [patients] in Flint—and maybe was never meant to.

Mona Hanna-Attisha, *What the Eyes Don't See*. New York: One World, 2018, p. 75.

home."[7] She eventually moved into the field of medical education, training new pediatricians to work with young patients, and then took a job as director of the pediatric residency program at Hurley Medical Center in Flint, Michigan. In 2011 she moved to Flint with her husband, Elliott Attisha, a fellow pediatrician, and the couple's two daughters, Nina and Layla.

Flint and the Water Crisis

Flint had once been a prosperous automobile manufacturing center, but by 2011 the industry had suffered setbacks and closures, and the city's financial base had declined. Coupled with the flight of the White middle class, the loss of manufacturing dollars meant that Flint's infrastructure also decayed. Both within Michigan and nationally, the city ranked near the bottom in most measures of health, wealth, and education. In 2011 Flint had the highest violent crime rate of any US city with over one hundred thousand people, and that rate remains high. Today about one

> "In a country riven by inequalities, Flint might be the place where the divide is most striking."[8]
>
> —Mona Hanna

in three Flint residents lives in poverty, and close to 20 percent of the homes citywide are abandoned. Moreover, just 35 percent of Flint's high school students graduate within four years. Perhaps most astonishing, the life expectancy for a child in Flint is fifteen years shorter than the expectancy for children in nearby communities. "In a country riven by inequalities," Hanna writes, "Flint might be the place where the divide is most striking."[8]

The lack of money was at the root of Flint's biggest problems. The city's population was falling, businesses were leaving, and the tax base was shrinking. Flint was having trouble paying its bills. To cut costs in 2013, the city opted to change the source of Flint's drinking water. Instead of drawing water from Lake Huron, one of the Great Lakes, Flint would pull its water from the nearby Flint River. The Flint River had been badly polluted earlier in its history, thanks largely to manufacturers dumping waste into its water, and had never been given a thorough

The Flint River had been badly polluted earlier in its history, thanks largely to manufacturers dumping waste into its water, and had never been given a thorough cleaning.

cleaning. Nevertheless, city administrators went ahead with the switch, expecting that the move would save the city several million dollars a year.

When the change was made in 2014, however, Flint residents complained bitterly. The water from the river seemed dirty when it arrived in people's homes. It was discolored, many people said, and smelled bad. "I won't let my dog drink it or my fish swim in it,"[9] said one woman who felt forced to buy bottled water for her household—an expense she and many other Flint residents could not easily afford. Bathing was an issue as well; people asserted that the water caused skin rashes. Still, Flint officials were unmoved. Despite its appearance, they argued, the water was harmless. "It's a quality, safe product," said the city's mayor. "I think people are wasting their precious money buying bottled water."[10]

But when a team of scientists from Virginia tested the water being pumped to homes and businesses, they found a serious issue: the water contained lead. Lead is useful in many

Talia and David Hanna

Mona Hanna is quite close to her parents, Talia and David. Indeed, she estimates that she talks to her mother on the phone at least twice a day. It is no surprise, then, that Mona's parents were especially powerful influences in her life and career. In particular, she credits them with instilling a love for education in her and her brother, along with the will to excel in whatever they were learning. "Doing schoolwork and getting good grades were expected by my Arab tiger mom," Hanna writes. "But in addition to what we learned in school, my parents urged us to read and learn independently about geography, history, literature, international affairs, and current events."

Besides emphasizing education, David and Talia spoke frequently to their children about activism and social justice. Hanna and her brother both learned from their parents to treat people with respect. Their parents also taught them the importance of standing up for what they believe is right. The lessons paid off. Both Mona and Mark have spent their careers helping people in need—Mark as a public interest lawyer in Washington, DC, and Mona as a pediatrician in Michigan.

Mona Hanna-Attisha, *What the Eyes Don't See*. New York: One World, 2018, p. 71.

manufacturing processes, but it is highly destructive when ingested by humans. That is especially true for babies and young children. "Effects include damage to the brain and nervous system and slowed growth and development," explains the Centers for Disease Control and Prevention, a government medical agency. "Children may also have learning and behavior problems and hearing and speech problems."[11] Worse yet, the effects of lead persist into later childhood, adolescence, and adulthood. Once lead has entered the body, there is no way to reverse its impact.

Even so, city and state officials continued to tell people that there was nothing to fear. "Anyone concerned about lead in the drinking water in Flint can relax,"[12] said a spokesperson for the Michigan Department of Environmental Quality. He claimed that lead affected only a few Flint homes and that most residents had nothing to worry about. Other officials argued that while lead dust and lead-based paint were dangerous, lead in water was not. Nonetheless, community activists remained unconvinced. They staged protests and tried to interest journalists in Flint's problems. But more than a year went by before any progress in the fight for safe water was made.

Scientific Evidence

That progress was due largely to the efforts of Hanna. Until August 2015 she had largely accepted officials' assurances that the water from the Flint River was safe. Then a friend who was an expert in water systems told her otherwise. "She said, 'Mona, the water isn't being treated properly,'" Hanna told a journalist. "'It's missing something called corrosion control. . . . Without that corrosion control, there is going to be lead.'"[13] Essentially, the water picked up lead as it traveled from the river through the pipes of Flint's water system. Adding corrosion coatings or chemical inhibitors would have eliminated the problem and cost the city less than $100 a day. But officials had elected to save the money and not add these controls to the water supply.

Because of her job, Hanna had access to the medical records of children who came to her hospital. Appalled by her friend's comments, she began a research study to look at the levels of lead in Flint's children. Within a month, Hanna and her research team had the results, and they were unsettling. Lead levels in the blood of the city's children had doubled since the shift to obtaining water from the Flint River. Moreover, the greatest increases in children's lead levels were in areas of the city where lead in the water was most common. Many children had levels of lead well above the maximum recommended by medical experts. Hanna shared her research with government officials in September 2015. "This is a crisis. This is an emergency,"[14] she told them.

Hanna was dismayed, however, when city and state officials not only rejected her findings but attacked her personally. "The state said that I was . . . causing near-hysteria, that I was splicing and dicing numbers," Hanna recalls. "It's very difficult when you are presenting science and facts and numbers to have the

Dr. Hanna speaks during a news conference about Flint water. Her research showed that the lead levels in children's blood had doubled since the city began obtaining water from the Flint River.

state say that you are wrong."[15] Though she wondered whether she was doing the right thing, she persevered. With the help of family and friends, along with other scientists and a coalition of community organizers, she won the battle. Later that month, city and state leaders backtracked and admitted that Hanna was right. The city swiftly returned to getting water from Lake Huron, though problems with lead remained; the problem may not be truly solved until all the city's pipes are replaced, which would cost an estimated $1.5 billion.

> "It's very difficult when you are presenting science and facts and numbers to have the state say that you are wrong."[15]
>
> —Mona Hanna

In the meantime, Hanna turned her attention to fighting the effects of lead on the children of Flint. Michigan's governor appointed her to the Michigan Child Lead Poisoning Elimination Board, which recommended testing of all the state's children for lead. She also organized a partnership of scientists and physicians to study ways to limit the damage done to children who have ingested lead. In addition, Hanna and other community members set up a fund to support children affected by the crisis and helped earmark millions of state and federal dollars to address the issues. Her book on the topic, *What the Eyes Don't See*, was published in 2018 and has also helped raise consciousness of the problems caused by lead.

Hanna Today

Today Hanna continues to be involved in medical care. As of 2024 she was an administrator in public health at Michigan State University. Her experience in Flint has also led her to fight childhood poverty, which she points out is connected to significant medical and psychological problems. Hanna's RX Kids program, funded partly by government and partly by private grants, provides money to mothers in Flint for the first year of their children's lives. Though this program is limited to Flint for now, Hanna insists that her work can be re-created in other communities. "It's about not being OK with babies growing up in poverty," she explains, and "about creating a replicable kind of playbook of how to do this in other places."[16]

Hanna has other interests as well. She embraces racial and cultural diversity and believes that the United States is stronger when its people come from varying backgrounds. Accordingly, she advocates for immigrants already in the United States and campaigns for immigration policies that will allow people from other countries to experience the benefits of America as she did. Still, Hanna is best known today for her work regarding the water crisis in Flint. And indeed, the role she played was central to the resolution of the crisis. As the host of a medical podcast puts it, Hanna's story is "amazing and heroic. . . . What would have happened to Flint if there wasn't a Dr. Mona to stand up and fight?"[17]

Hoda Kotb, Broadcast Journalist

Of all Middle Eastern American women, Hoda Kotb is perhaps the most immediately recognizable. That is due to her many years of work in television. After holding positions as a news anchor and reporter in local stations, Kotb took a job as a reporter on the popular NBC news show *Dateline*. Her work on this series made her face and voice familiar to millions of Americans. More recently, Kotb has hosted and anchored NBC's morning program *The Today Show*. She has won awards and honors for her work both as a reporter and as an anchor, and even though she announced that she would be stepping down from broadcast journalism in early 2025, she will likely remain one of the country's best-known—and best-loved—television personalities.

Growing Up

Hoda Kotb was born in Norman, Oklahoma, in 1964 to parents who immigrated to the United States from Cairo, Egypt. Hoda's father, Abdel, was a mining engineer who was employed in the oil industry, and her mother, Sameha, worked as a nursing assistant and later joined the staff at the Library of Congress in Washington, DC. Kotb's family also included an older sister, Hala, and a younger brother, Adel. The Kotb family focused much less on their Egyptian roots than on their status as Americans. "My parents were so proud to be American citizens," Kotb remembered years later. "They dressed

More recently in her long career, Hoda Kotb has hosted and anchored NBC's morning program The Today Show.

in the current styles and demanded we speak English as our first language. . . . We were United States citizens and were taught to never consider ourselves different."[18]

Young Hoda did not remain in Oklahoma for long. Shortly before she began kindergarten, Abdel and Sameha moved the family to Morgantown, West Virginia. Kotb's time in Morgantown did not always go smoothly. She did not feel connected to her neighbors and classmates at first. "When you have a weird name and your hair and skin are different, and you don't blend in, it's a long year," she recalled as an adult. "You have to work extra hard to make friends."[19] Indeed, Kotb remembered trying so hard not to be noticed that she rarely spoke above a whisper in school.

When Hoda was ten, the Kotb family moved again—this time to Nigeria in West Africa, a center of the global oil industry. This move was an enormous shock to Kotb. Nigerian customs struck her as wildly different from what she had experienced in the United States. "All the boys had three tribal scars raked into their faces," Kotb remembers about her first day of fifth grade, "and the girls had their hair wrapped in thin wire that was then bent backward." She was appalled, moreover, to discover that her Nigerian teacher hit students simply for asking questions. But Kotb eventually made friends and grew comfortable in her new home. "We learned that not everybody looks and sounds the same," she explains in her autobiography. "I think that's a terrific lesson for kids."[20]

> **"My parents were so proud to be American citizens. They dressed in the current styles and demanded we speak English as our first language."[18]**
>
> —Hoda Kotb

After two years in Africa the family returned briefly to West Virginia and then moved to Alexandria, Virginia, outside Washington, DC. Kotb spent the remainder of her childhood and adolescence in Alexandria, graduating from high school in 1982 and attending Virginia Polytechnic Institute—also known as Virginia Tech—for college. But while the Kotbs spent most of the year in Virginia, they traveled to Egypt each summer to visit family members. Kotb recalls particularly the fun of playing with her cousins. "Egypt was a blast," she wrote years later. "Imagine, as a kid, having the exotic pyramids as a playground. We . . . rode camels and donkeys and played in our infinity sandbox [the Sahara Desert]."[21] Once again, Kotb was being exposed to a large and diverse world.

Broadcast Journalism

Kotb graduated from Virginia Tech in 1986 with a degree in communications. Her main interest in this field was broadcast journalism. Although one of her professors predicted that she would not be successful in this industry, Kotb set out to find a position in television news. Deciding to begin job hunting in Egypt rather than in America, Kotb eventually landed an entry-level role with CBS in Cairo. Kotb was given few responsibilities at first. Indeed, she later described the job as a combination of "getting coffee and getting yelled at."[22] Still, Kotb did occasionally appear on air,

Eligible Bachelors

For the most part, Hoda Kotb loved going to Egypt during the summers when she was growing up. Her positive experiences helped her make the decision to start her journalism career there rather than in the United States. But there was one thing about Egypt that Kotb found annoying. To her it seemed that family members were constantly trying to match her with young men for the purpose of dating and possible marriage. In her autobiography, Kotb summed up her relatives' attempts to interest her in potential husbands as follows: "Hoda, someone's at the door for yoooo-ouuuu. . . . This is Mohammed. He's from Cairo. He's studying engineering . . . and he has a Mercedes." The relatives may have been well meaning, but Kotb refused to play along. "I wanted nothing to do with any of [the men]," she recalls. "Plus, never tell me what to do. Bad approach."

Hoda Kotb, *Hoda*. New York: Simon & Schuster, 2010, pp. 17–18.

and when she moved back to the United States a year later, she was confident of finding work.

She was wrong. Kotb borrowed her mother's car and drove it across the South in search of a job. Though her travels took her to television stations in multiple states, a total of twenty-seven news directors turned her down. Then, after taking a wrong turn in Mississippi, Kotb saw a billboard advertising a station located in the city of Greenville—one that she had originally dismissed as being in too small a market. Now, however, Kotb thought otherwise. "I figured, *What did I have to lose?*" she remembered afterward. "I drove to Greenville, digging deep for one last shred of hope." The news director, Stan Sandroni, saw something promising in Kotb and offered her a job. As Kotb put it years later, "My wrong turn turned out to be one of the best mistakes I've ever made."[23]

"My wrong turn turned out to be one of the best mistakes I've ever made."[23]

—Hoda Kotb

Kotb began by reporting on various news items in and around Greenville, appearing briefly on camera when her stories were deemed important enough. However, Kotb wanted to be an anchor—the person who hosts the broadcast. She got the chance when the regular newsreader was out sick. Sandroni asked who in the office had a blazer. When Kotb said she did, Sandroni assigned her to substitute. Kotb immediately flubbed her first line, wishing her viewers a good morning even though it was evening. Still, Sandroni was forgiving and soon promoted her to full-time anchor for the station's five o'clock news show.

For Kotb, the Greenville position was just the first of several successful television jobs. She worked for two years in Moline, Illinois, then moved on to Fort Myers, Florida, and finally took a job in the large market of New Orleans, Louisiana. Kotb thoroughly enjoyed New Orleans, but after six years she caught the attention of Elena Nachmanoff, a vice president at NBC News. Nachmanoff invited Kotb to apply for a job reporting for a news show called *Dateline*, which would mean relocating to NBC network headquarters in New York City. Kotb was thrilled. "Your whole life you dream of the network!" she said at the time. "Who doesn't dream of the network?"[24] NBC executives hired her after watching her audition tape. In early 1998 Kotb moved to New York and began work as a correspondent for *Dateline*.

Dateline and *The Today Show*

Kotb served as a full-time reporter for *Dateline* for close to ten years. Her time on the show was eventful. She traveled frequently to chase down important news stories; Kotb's work took her to foreign locations such as Pakistan, Iraq, and Thailand as well as to cities and towns in the United States. Several of her news stories won her praise from viewers and television professionals. Domestically, for example, Kotb reported on the struggles and triumphs of a first-year teacher in Georgia. Her resulting report, "The Education of Ms. Groves," earned Kotb and her crew two major awards given for excellence in broadcast journalism in 2005. The story "struck a nerve," recalls Kotb. "It made people feel something."[25] Later in 2005, Kotb returned to New Orleans to report on Hurricane Katrina, a disastrous storm that devastated the city.

War Zones

During her career as a broadcast journalist, Hoda Kotb was sent across the world to give reports. Some of the locations she visited were safe. Others were not. The danger was especially strong during Kotb's visits to Afghanistan in 2002 and Iraq a year later.

Kotb's trip to Afghanistan was during Operation Enduring Freedom, a long-running series of hostilities between Afghan rulers and the US military. Kotb recalls seeing signs of warfare all over the capital city of Kabul, including tanks and buildings damaged by the shooting. Moreover, hundreds of land mines were buried along roads leading into town. "The region was infested with them," she remembers. Fortunately, neither Kotb nor any members of her news crew suffered injuries on the trip.

Kotb also escaped injury in Iraq, where she was sent shortly after the country was invaded by US troops. Though the invasion was successful, guerrilla violence persisted throughout much of Iraq while Kotb was there. Kotb remembers hearing steady gunfire, especially during her time in Baghdad, the nation's capital. She was astonished to learn that many Iraqis and even some journalists covering the war were able to ignore the sounds of the shots because they were so frequent.

Hoda Kotb, *Hoda*. New York: Simon & Schuster, 2010, p. 82.

Kotb's foreign *Dateline* reports were also well received. In 2000 she traveled to Myanmar in Southeast Asia to interview Aung San Suu Kyi, a political prisoner who had received a Nobel Prize for her efforts to bring peace to the world. Because the government of Myanmar refused to allow foreign journalists to interview Suu Kyi, Kotb and her producer had to pretend they were ordinary tourists. Antigovernment agents helped smuggle them into a meeting with Suu Kyi, and Kotb and her producer hid the tapes of the interview in false compartments within their shoes. It was the first interview with Suu Kyi in eleven years.

During her time on *Dateline*, Kotb occasionally reported for other shows on NBC and its allied stations. For a time she hosted a series called *Your Total Health*. In 2007 she began appearing on the popular and successful *The Today Show*, broadcast each weekday morning across America. Her first assignment was to be cohost of the last hour of each episode, which typically featured relatively light topics such as health, exercise, and beauty. However, Kotb was eventually given the responsibility of coanchoring the entire show, reminding her of her roots in Greenville many years earlier.

A Medical Crisis

Though 2007 brough Kotb the thrill of joining *The Today Show*, it also brought stress and sorrow. That year her marriage to a New Orleans tennis coach named Burzis Kanga ended in divorce. Moreover, Kotb was diagnosed with breast cancer in 2007. She had surgery to remove the tumors and took medications to prevent their reoccurrence. Both treatments were effective—Kotb has been cancer-free ever since—but the medicine she took left her infertile. Nonetheless, Kotb considers herself fortunate. "No radiation for me," she wrote in her autobiography, "no chemotherapy." Still, the experience taught Kotb that people did not discuss breast cancer nearly enough. "All I can do," she wrote, "is focus on the fact that perhaps I have a platform to do *something* about it."[26]

Kotb speaks at a breast cancer awareness event. Since her cancer diagnosis and recovery in 2007, she has been a prominent advocate for breast cancer research and awareness.

She did just that. In an episode of *The Today Show* broadcast in late 2007, Kotb discussed her cancer, surgery, and prognosis. Her goal was to raise awareness of breast cancer and urge women to have regular breast exams. Following the broadcast, she received many positive messages from viewers across the country. Since then, the show has featured Kotb talking about her experience with cancer on multiple occasions. In 2024, for example, she spoke of becoming emotionally stronger after the diagnosis and the operation to remove the tumor. "I feel like your life does snap into focus," she said. "I think I realized my life was short and limited and I should ask for what I wanted."[27]

Although Kotb was no longer able to bear children after her surgery, she nevertheless wanted to be a mother. In 2017 she and her partner, Joel Schiffman, adopted a baby girl, whom they named Haley Joy, and two years later the couple adopted a second daughter, Hope Catherine. "They put [Haley] in my arms," Kotb explained on a 2021 podcast. "She fit like she was born there. I looked down and those eyes were looking at me and I thought to myself, 'Forever, for as long as I am breathing, you will be protected and loved and cared for.'"[28] Kotb and Schiffman are no longer a couple, but Kotb says that they continue to work well together as coparents. Kotb also remains close to her extended family, including her siblings and their children along with her mother, and she cherishes the memory of her father, who died when Kotb was in college.

Going Forward

In addition to her work as a television personality and her focus on breast cancer awareness, Kotb has been involved in other projects during her career. Perhaps most notably, she is an author with multiple books to her credit. In 2010 she published *Hoda*, an autobiography cowritten with author Jane Lorenzini. Three years later she again partnered with Lorenzini to write a book called *Ten Years Later*, which highlights six people who overcame serious illnesses, abusive relationships, and other adversities. And she has

In addition to her work as a television personality and her focus on breast cancer awareness, Kotb is also an author with multiple books to her credit.

written several children's books, among them *Hope Is a Rainbow*, which was released in 2024.

Though Kotb spent close to two decades as an integral member of *The Today Show*, she announced that she would step down in early 2025. As of early 2025, it was not clear what she would do next, but she does intend to keep active and busy with

"[Kotb's] warmth, laughter, and incredible spirit have brightened our mornings and touched countless hearts."[30]

—Kathie Lee Gifford, television personality

new projects. "I love new adventures,"[29] she said in an interview shortly after making her announcement. Whatever she decides, Kotb has created an impressive legacy in broadcast journalism. She has won multiple awards for her work, and she has been nominated for many other honors as well. Perhaps most important, Kotb has had a positive impact on millions of Americans over the years. From Greenville and New Orleans to New York City, viewers across the country have appreciated Kotb's honesty, humor, and compassion. Kathie Lee Gifford, Kotb's former cohost on *The Today Show*, spoke for many when she wrote of her colleague, "Her warmth, laughter, and incredible spirit have brightened our mornings and touched countless hearts."[30]

Rima Fakih, Miss USA

Few Middle Eastern American women have been involved in as many different types of activities as Rima Fakih. Fakih—also known by her married name, Rima Fakih Slaiby—is a Lebanese American who is most famous for being a beauty pageant winner. In 2010 she broke new ground when she became the first immigrant Arab American to win the Miss USA beauty contest. However, Fakih has also drawn attention in more recent years for other activities. That includes a connection with WWE, also known as World Wrestling Entertainment. In addition to crowning champions during televised WWE events, Fakih trained to improve her own athletic skills with a view toward becoming a professional wrestler herself. Though her career as a participant was short lived, Fakih is proud of her association with WWE. She is certainly one of the few American beauty pageant winners to also appear in the wrestling ring.

Besides serving as Miss USA and connecting with professional wrestling, Fakih has been a frequent guest star on television programs and has appeared on multiple reality shows. She is also an advocate for many charitable causes. She has used her status as a pageant winner and celebrity to raise money for programs that combat homelessness, feed the hungry, fund cancer research, and assist people with developmental disabilities, among many other causes. Most of Fakih's philanthropic activities benefit people in the United States, but some have been designed to help the people of Lebanon, the

In 2010 Rima Fakih became the first immigrant Arab American to win the Miss USA beauty contest. Since then, Fakih has also participated in other activities.

country where Fakih was born and lived until age eight. "Our hearts are deeply embedded in our homeland of Lebanon,"[31] Fakih and her husband, Wassim, wrote in 2020.

War and Emigration

Rima Fakih was born in 1985 in Srifa, a small town in the southern part of Lebanon. She was one of five children—three girls and two boys—born to Nadia and Hussein Fakih. Rima came into the world during a drawn-out civil war that devastated Lebanon. That war affected every part of the country, badly damaged Lebanon's economy, and deeply divided its people. In particular, the war pitted Christian elites against the majority Muslim population. From its origins in 1975 to its end in 1990, the war caused the deaths of about 150,000 Lebanese.

"Our hearts are deeply embedded in our homeland of Lebanon."[31]

—Rima Fakih

In addition to these casualties, the civil war also led to the emigration of approximately 1 million Lebanese, or roughly 40 percent of the country's population. Most of those who left were looking for political or economic stability elsewhere. Many settled in nearby Arab countries such as Syria or Egypt. Others came to the Americas, finding new homes in nations such as Brazil, Argentina, and the United States. Free elections were finally held in 1992, two years following the close of the war, but the damage done to the economy—and to the trust among the groups that populated Lebanon—meant that the exodus continued.

The Fakih family tried to stay out of the conflict as much as possible. Though they were Muslims, they bore no ill will toward the Christian population and appreciated the contributions made by people of all religions to their country. But staying neutral was difficult. "We [didn't] take sides," recalled Rima's sister Rana Faqih years afterward, "and this is strange in a country like Lebanon."[32] Distrusted by Christians and Muslims alike, the Fakih family joined the flight from their homeland. In 1993, when Rima was eight years old, she and her family moved to Queens, a borough of New York City. Her father and his brothers opened a Mediterranean restaurant in nearby Manhattan.

For some time, things were looking up for the Fakihs. Rima attended a Catholic high school in Queens and settled into life in the United States. But on September 11, 2001, terrorists from the extreme Islamist group al Qaeda killed nearly three thousand people after hijacking four passenger airplanes and crashing them into buildings in New York and the Pentagon, as well as a field in Virginia. Though only one of the terrorists was Lebanese, with the great majority coming from Saudi Arabia, many Americans did not focus on the exact nationalities of the hijackers in the wake of the attacks. Instead, they blamed Muslims and the Arab world in general for the violence. Muslims in many parts of the United States reported being threatened and feeling unsafe.

No one in the Fakih family was physically injured following the terrorist strikes, but Rima's parents perceived a change in New Yorkers' attitudes toward them. Business at Hussein Fakih's restaurant dropped off, a decline that family members attributed to anger over the September 11 attacks. In 2003 the family closed the restaurant, left New York, and moved to Dearborn, a city just outside Detroit in southeastern Michigan. Dearborn was the center of a vibrant Arab American community, representing the largest concentration of people of Arab heritage in the United States. The Fakihs hoped to find a warm welcome in Michigan and leave behind the distrustful attitudes that they had experienced in Queens.

Early Pageants

Dearborn was all they had hoped for, and Rima Fakih thrived following her family's move. "The strength of my family and our unity led me to become fearless," she recalled years later. "I felt no boundaries when it came to getting things done."[33] She initially continued her education by enrolling in community college and later earned a degree in business management and economics from the University of Michigan–Dearborn. After graduation, Fakih took a job working in the development office of the Detroit Medical Center. Her duties included fundraising as well as reaching out to Arab Americans in the Detroit-Dearborn area.

"The strength of my family and our unity led me to become fearless. I felt no boundaries when it came to getting things done."[33]

—Rima Fakih

At the same time, however, Fakih had developed a new interest. Encouraged by her mother, Fakih entered her first beauty pageant when she was nineteen. This was the Miss Wayne County contest—one of the qualifying competitions for women eager to earn the title of Miss Michigan and compete for the title of Miss America, the most prestigious beauty pageant in the United States. Fakih did not become Miss Wayne County, but her fifth-place finish in the contest represented a strong showing, and she decided to take part in more pageants in the years to come.

Dearborn, Detroit, and Arab Americans

The Detroit region in southeastern Michigan is home to more than four hundred thousand Middle Eastern Americans. Indeed, by most estimates the Detroit metro area has more people with Middle Eastern ancestry than any other in the United States, including much more populous urban areas such as New York City and Los Angeles. Middle Eastern Americans are especially numerous in Dearborn, the city to which Rima Fakih and her family moved after leaving New York. In 2023 more than half of Dearborn's 110,000 residents were of Middle Eastern background.

Like Fakih and her family, many of the Middle Eastern Americans in southeastern Michigan have roots in Lebanon. Though some Lebanese lived in the region in the late 1800s, the first major wave of Lebanese immigrants to the area arrived in the 1920s. This was a prosperous decade in which car manufacturers based in the region were looking for workers. Several thousand Lebanese left the Middle East at the time and found jobs in automobile factories. Today many Lebanese continue to migrate to Detroit and settle alongside other immigrants from Iraq, Yemen, and Palestine.

In 2008 Fakih learned of a pageant for Lebanese women who no longer lived in their home country. This pageant was sponsored by the World Lebanese Cultural Union, an international organization that promotes Lebanese art, music, and traditions. The winner would return to Lebanon the following year to compete for the title of Miss Lebanon. Fakih met the qualifications, which included "high educational level," "height around 170 centimeters," and "single or divorced without having children,"[34] and she entered the pageant. She did quite well in the competition, too, placing third behind contestants from Brazil and Australia.

Miss USA

Proud of doing so well in these first pageants, Fakih entered a new contest in 2009. This one was designed to crown Miss USA, a title sought after by women from across the country. All fifty states, along with the District of Columbia, hold their own pageants to choose the woman who will represent them in the Miss USA competition. The Miss USA winner goes on to compete in an international pageant known as Miss Universe. In late 2009 Fakih won the state contest for Michigan, earning her the title of Miss Michigan USA and the opportunity to compete for the national title in 2010. That May she beat out fifty other contestants to win the title of Miss USA. That made her the first Lebanese American woman to hold the title.

Fakih was overjoyed. "I'm living like a queen right now,"[35] she said shortly after the pageant was over. Her friends and family

Some Muslims were appalled that Fakih would participate in a beauty contest in which women appear in bikini swimwear. In their view, Islam requires women to cover more of their bodies in public.

> "To say that she is a Muslim is inaccurate. No Muslim woman can call herself a . . . Muslim and be on stage [in] her bikini."[38]
>
> —Ghazal Omid, Canadian scholar and writer

were equally delighted. "I was so proud, as an Arab-American and a Michigander,"[36] said her friend Sueheila Amen, and Rima's sister Rana called the news "a beautiful surprise."[37] Even the mayor of Srifa, the town where Fakih was born, expressed his appreciation. Fakih immediately began her duties as the new Miss USA, which included attending public events in person throughout the country as well as appearing on television. Like all Miss USAs, Fakih had causes she promoted during her year as titleholder: she advocated for women's self-defense training and worked to educate women about breast and ovarian cancer.

Not everyone was equally pleased with Fakih's win, however. Some Muslims were appalled that Fakih would participate in a beauty contest—in which women appear in swimwear—and still think of herself as devout. In their view, Islam requires women to cover more of their bodies in public. "To say that she is a Muslim is inaccurate," charged Ghazal Omid, a Canadian scholar and writer. "No Muslim woman can call herself a . . . Muslim and be on stage [in] her bikini."[38] Fakih and her supporters, however, pointed out that there are many different interpretations of Islam and that she and her family have never been associated with the more conservative elements of the faith. "Religion does not identify me," she told an interviewer. "We are Muslim, however, we appreciate and admire all faiths."[39]

New Interests

Fakih went on to compete in the Miss Universe pageant later in 2010, but she did not reach the semifinals. She remained in the public eye, however. In the next few years, Fakih appeared on television multiple times, including talk shows such as *Good Morning America* and late-night shows hosted by comedians David Letterman and Jimmy Fallon. She also guested on reality television, including an episode of *The Choice*, a dating game show; an appearance in the Middle Eastern version of the series

Hezbollah

Hezbollah is a political and paramilitary organization based in Lebanon and supported by the Iranian government. It opposes the right of Israel to exist, and it resists Western powers that operate in the Middle East. Because of its frequent use of violence, many countries—including the United States—consider it a terrorist group.

When Rima Fakih won the Miss USA title, some conservative commentators charged that Fakih supported Hezbollah and its activities. One right-wing blogger, Debbie Schlussel, referred to Fakih as "Miss Hezbollah USA" and added that "Hezbollah . . . won the Miss USA contest." Schlussel and others believed, moreover, that Fakih was receiving money from Hezbollah. "Her bid for the pageant," Schlussel wrote, "was financed by an Islamic terrorist."

Fakih and her supporters were quick to deny any connection between Fakih or her family and Hezbollah. Experts on Hezbollah also dismissed the notion that Fakih and the organization were linked. Indeed, the accusations were baseless and seem to have been founded largely on Islamophobia rather than on any real-world evidence.

Quoted in Alexandra Sandels, "Lebanon: First Muslim Miss USA Winner Derided as 'Miss Hezbollah USA' by Conservatives." *Los Angeles Times*, May 18, 2010. www.latimes.com.

Dancing with the Stars; and a series produced and broadcast in Asia called *The Apartment—Celebrity Edition*. In addition, she has appeared on the covers of many magazines in the United States, Lebanon, Vietnam, India, and Italy.

But beyond her beauty pageant experience, Fakih may be best known for her connection with professional wrestling. As Miss USA she made many appearances at wrestling events. The most notable of these took place in November 2010, when she served as a guest star on a program called *WWE Raw* and crowned the champion of the King of the Ring tournament. In 2012 she was a featured guest at a wrestling fan convention called WrestleMania Axxess. She also became interested in competing as a wrestler herself, at a time when the great majority of wrestlers were men. Her career as a competitor was short, but she did take part in a show called *WWE Tough Enough V*, a reality series in which competitors were cut from the show depending on their attitude or performance. Fakih was eliminated in the fourth episode.

Since her wrestling career came to an end, Fakih has focused primarily on philanthropy. She has remained dedicated to promoting cancer awareness and women's self-defense while also participating in fundraising efforts for organizations that make a positive impact both in the United States and globally. Together with celebrities Brandy and Vivica A. Fox, for example, Fakih raised $450,000 in 2022 for Best Buddies International, which advocates for people with intellectual and developmental disabilities. She has also been active in programs such as School on Wheels, which educates homeless children in Los Angeles. "Currently we have 163,000 homeless kids in Los Angeles County," Fakih said in 2022. "That is not an easy number to take in."[40]

Following a disaster in Lebanon in 2020, Fakih and her husband started a fundraising campaign called Global Aid for Lebanon which raised $1.2 million in just over a week.

Fakih's philanthropy also extends to her birth country. In 2020, for example, Lebanon suffered a devastating explosion in the capital city of Beirut. Over two hundred people were killed, many more were injured, and property damage was widespread. Following the disaster, Fakih and her husband started a fundraising campaign called Global Aid for Lebanon; they raised $1.2 million in just over a week. On a lighter note, in 2018 Fakih took on the challenge of running the Miss Lebanon 2018 beauty pageant. This task combined her knowledge of business with her experience as a participant—and winner—in other contests.

Today, Fakih lives in Los Angeles with her family. Her husband, Wassim Slaiby, nicknamed Sal, is a Lebanese Canadian music producer and entrepreneur; the couple married in 2016 in Lebanon. Before marrying Slaiby, a Christian, Fakih officially converted from Islam to Christianity; she and her husband are members of an Eastern Catholic group called the Maronite Church. The couple has four children: Rima, Joseph, Amira, and Jacob. In her spare time, Fakih enjoys binge-watching television shows, journaling, and cooking. Though she has chosen to live in America, Fakih continues to see her Lebanese roots as vital to understanding the trajectory of her life—including whatever may come. As she likes to say, "You don't know who you are until you know where you come from."[41]

CHAPTER FOUR

Adah Almutairi, Nanoscientist

The prefix *nano-* means "one-billionth." Thus, a nanometer is a unit of measurement equal to one-billionth of a meter. To find objects that measure one nanometer or less, it is necessary to look at atoms and molecules—the building blocks of all matter. Scientists who deal with matter at the nanoscale—that is, at dimensions of less than one hundred nanometers—discover that it behaves in unexpected ways compared to more familiar objects (which are often known as bulk materials to distinguish them from the nanoscale). Compared to bulk materials, for instance, some materials at nanoscale have unusual magnetic properties, while others change their melting point, improve their ability to conduct electricity, or react differently with other materials. The study of materials at nanoscale is often referred to as nanoscience, and scientists and inventors who find uses for these incredibly small materials are engaged in nanotechnology.

Nanoscience has many uses in the modern world. Computer circuits, for example, are built using nanotechnology. Sunscreens use nanoparticles of zinc or other materials to block ultraviolet radiation, and clothing manufacturers make use of nanotechnology to make their product more water-resistant. But perhaps the most significant use of nanotechnology in modern times is in the field of medicine. Nanotechnology has been used to build medical devices, help diagnose illness, and heal the body. Many Americans have been involved in the effort to use tiny materials to improve medical care, and one of the most prominent is a Middle Eastern American scientist and inventor named Adah Almutairi.

From the Middle East to California

Adah Almutairi was born in Portland, Oregon, in 1976. Her parents, Mutlaq and Najat, had left Saudi Arabia for Oregon so that Mutlaq, Adah's father, could study criminology. Upon completing his degree, Mutlaq moved his family back to Saudi Arabia, where he worked as a police investigator. Despite living in a country where girls often were kept from pursuing educational opportunities, Mutlaq valued schooling for all five of his children, including his daughters. Mutlaq encountered fierce opposition from his own family when he announced his intention to have Adah get an education. "My father and grandfather got into a lot of fights," Almutairi recalled years afterward, "because my grandfather did not believe women should be educated."[42]

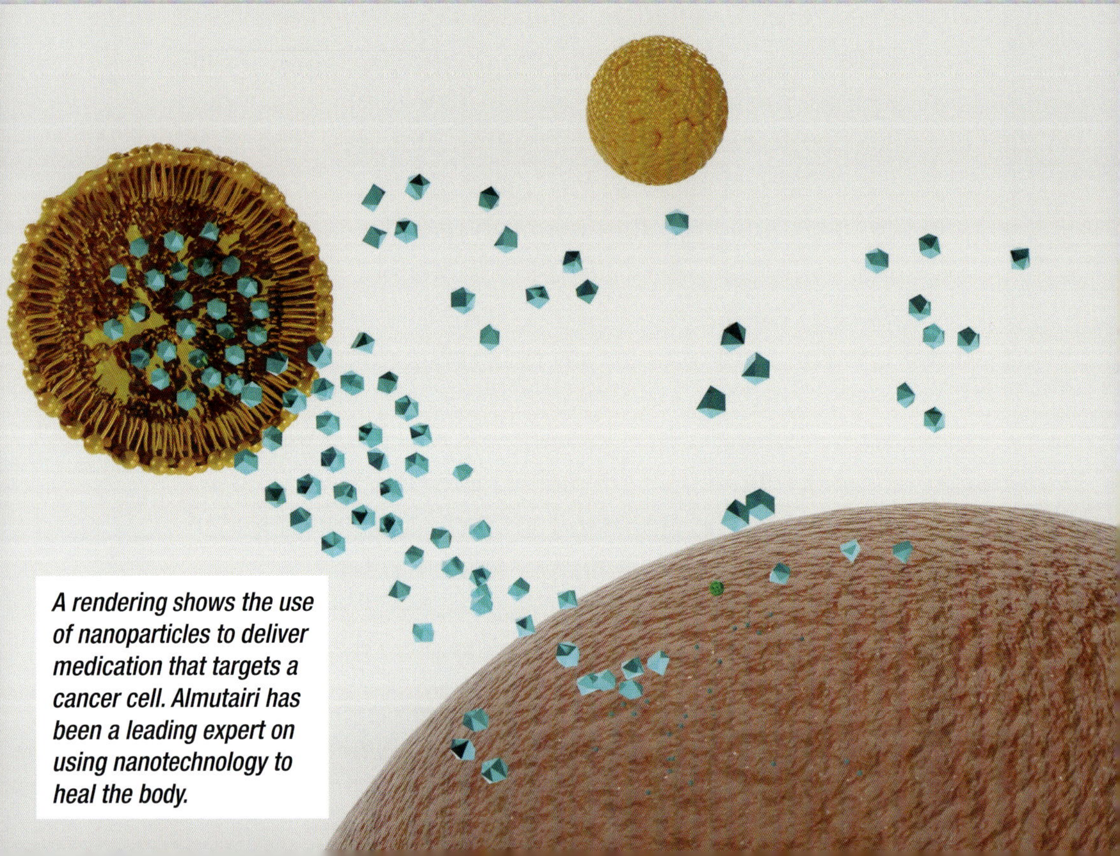

A rendering shows the use of nanoparticles to deliver medication that targets a cancer cell. Almutairi has been a leading expert on using nanotechnology to heal the body.

> "My father and grandfather got into a lot of fights, because my grandfather did not believe women should be educated."[42]
>
> —Adah Almutairi

Adah's father, however, prevailed and enrolled Adah in international schools in Saudi Arabia. She excelled both academically and athletically. Her favorite subjects were science and math, and she was part of her high school gymnastics and track teams. Her athletic career, however, got off to a difficult start. At her first gymnastics meet, young Adah did not perform up to her standards. Embarrassed by her mistakes, especially since they had come in front of an audience of family and friends, Adah broke down in tears. However, she resolved to do better in the future by focusing more on practice and preparation. Her hard work paid off, and she became a top performer in both of her sports.

Almutairi finished high school at age sixteen. Uncertain what to do next, she applied for a job teaching English at an all-girls' school in Riyadh, Saudi Arabia's capital. To her surprise, she got the job even though she lacked a college degree—or any college education at all. "When the headmistress realised how young I was," Almutairi recalled years later, "she said: 'Don't tell anyone, just put some lipstick on.'" As a teacher, Almutairi especially enjoyed bringing in copies of *Reader's Digest* magazines belonging to her mother and having students carry out writing exercises based on their contents. "It was the best job ever," Almutairi recalls. "I loved every minute. I had such a connection with the girls."[43]

> "[Teaching school] was the best job ever. I loved every minute. I had such a connection with the girls."[43]
>
> —Adah Almutairi

Before long, though, Almutairi decided to further her own education. She applied to King Abdulaziz University, the largest school in Saudi Arabia and among the most prestigious, but she did not get in. She then set her sights on an American school, Occidental College in Los Angeles, California, which not only admitted her but gave her an athletic scholarship. Almutairi's grandfather bitterly opposed the idea that she should attend college, especially by moving to the United States—and by traveling there on her own—but Mutlaq overruled his father again. Almutairi began her studies at Occidental College in 1996.

Her parents hoped she would study medicine, but Almutairi had other ideas. Initially focusing on math, she switched to chemistry midway through her second year in college. The switch was partly due to her own realization that she enjoyed the concepts and experiments associated with chemistry. It also had to do with the influence of Tetsuo Otsuki, a chemistry professor at Occidental, who encouraged her to study the subject. "He made me feel smart and capable, and worth being taught,"[44] she recalls. Upon graduation from Occidental in 2000, Almutairi won a fellowship to attend graduate school in chemistry at the University of California, Riverside. She entered the program that fall.

An Academic Career

Although Almutairi enjoyed her graduate studies, she was not sure what she wanted to do with her degree. Chemists often work in labs at large pharmaceutical companies or for other manufacturers, but Almutairi's graduate adviser steered her away from the corporate world. She impressed him with her intelligence and curiosity, and he convinced her to become a scholar instead. "I couldn't imagine you doing anything outside of academic work,"[45] he told her. Almutairi needed little convincing. She graduated from Riverside with a doctorate in 2015. Her specialty was the study of electrons and molecules. It was her first major venture into the world of tiny materials.

Beginning in 2005 Almutairi did further study in chemistry and chemical engineering at the University of California, Berkeley. During this time her interest in nanotechnology began to blossom. In conjunction with her mentor, Berkeley professor Jean Fréchet, she did research into the field of in vivo imaging, a three-dimensional system allowing scientists to look deep inside living animals to diagnose and track the progression of disease. In vivo imaging uses tiny fluorescent particles to identify tumors and other medical problems. With Fréchet, Almutairi published several papers on in vivo

Nanotechnology and Vision

One important procedure Almutairi developed with her team at the University of California, San Diego, focused on treatments related to the eyes. Some vision-related conditions require patients to undergo regular injections of drugs directly into the back of the eye. This procedure, however, is problematic. "It's very invasive," points out Almutairi, "and the more injections you have, the greater your risk of scarring and retinal damage." The risk to patients is compounded by the possibility that doctors inexperienced with the method may miss their target; as Almutairi delicately puts it, "Not just anyone can poke you in the eye."

Working with an ophthalmologist, Almutairi developed a molecule that can be placed into the eye and release medication as needed. Though replacing the molecule is still an invasive procedure, it typically needs to be done only once a year. Almutairi's technique has been used in clinics and hospitals and has helped prevent blindness in people whose retinas are beginning to fail.

Quoted in Rachel Nuwer, "Light Therapy," *Slate*, March 8, 2015. https://slate.com.

imaging and its connection to nanotechnology and health. The in vivo system was not perfect—there were concerns about whether the technology involved was safe for human beings, for example, along with questions about the cost of the materials needed to carry out the process—but Fréchet and Almutairi helped advance the development of in vivo imaging, bringing it closer to becoming a reality.

While working with Fréchet, Almutairi also presented her research to audiences of chemists and other scientists. Though they found her ideas intriguing, they typically expressed doubt that her work was of any practical benefit. She says she was often told, "That's elegant chemistry. But there will never be useful, human applications for this sort of thing."[46] Undeterred, Almutairi and Fréchet continued their research while trying to convince others that nanotechnology could indeed be useful in improving human lives. As Almutairi likes to point out, knowledge is valuable even when it may not be immediately clear what impact a particular process or device may have. "We want to give these tools

"We want to give these tools to biologists and see all the ways they find to use it. Inventors are often surprised by the application of their own work."[47]

—Adah Almutairi

to biologists and see all the ways they find to use it," she says. "Inventors are often surprised by the application of their own work."[47]

In 2008 Almutairi began looking for a permanent position in the academic world. Unable to find a job in Saudi Arabia, which would have been her first choice, she instead accepted an offer from the University of California, San Diego (UCSD) as an assistant professor. She became known for her eagerness to work with people from other scientific disciplines and before long became the head of a research group at UCSD's Center for Excellence in Nanomedicine and Engineering. This work combined several of her deepest interests—

In 2008, Almutairi accepted an offer as an assistant professor from the Jacobs School of Engineering at UCSD. She soon became the head of a research group in nanomedicine.

engineering, nanotechnology, and medicine—and she began developing products that did indeed have a clear value to human beings. She also began filing for patents for some of these new products, which she developed with other researchers from UCSD.

Medical Technology

Indeed, as Almutairi continued her research at UCSD, she was increasingly able to find uses for the nanotechnologies she was investigating. For example, filling nanoparticles with medications that fight cancer proved an effective extension of the in vivo imaging Almutairi was researching with Fréchet. These nanoparticles hold tiny amounts of water in addition to the anticancer drugs. First, the particles are injected into the tissues of the body where they will do the most good. Then, light beams from a low-powered laser are trained on the particles. The light rays heat the water and dissolve the exterior of the nanoparticle, allowing the release of the drugs within. Healthy tissue that would be harmed by the drug will not be affected by the medication's release, since the particles reach only the unhealthy tissue. In addition to its uses in medicine, Almutairi notes that the process could also be used to make light-activated sunscreens or to regulate the amounts of pesticides used in agriculture.

One of Almutairi's practical applications was developed in tandem with her brother Khalid, a plastic surgeon. This discovery involved the process of liposuction, a method of removing fat from the human body. The genesis of Almutairi's idea came from her own concern with her weight. "I had about 10 lb to lose," Almutairi recalls of a vacation she took soon after giving birth to her son. She remembers thinking, "If only I could melt this fat so I could wear a bathing suit tomorrow."[48] Traditional liposuction, in which an incision is made and fat is essentially vacuumed out of the body, was for years the standard way of removing excess fat. However, Almutairi knew that this technique often causes bruising and damages healthy tissue or nerves, and many people are as a result reluctant to undergo the procedure.

Almutairi lost the weight she wanted through exercise and healthy eating, but her desire for something that could melt fat led her to a realization based on her research. She theorized that nanoparticles made of gold might be helpful in melting deposits of fat in the body. The procedure would be similar to the light-activated cancer treatment. Infrared light from a laser would be aimed at the gold nanoparticles injected into the body. The light would heat the gold and melt the surrounding fat. The melted fat would then be suctioned out of the body with a needle, with little if any damage to the rest of the body

When Almutairi returned home, she consulted with Khalid, who urged her to do further research to see whether she could make her idea a reality. Almutairi soon began running experiments in which she injected gold nanoparticles into two foods known for their fat content—butter and bacon—and then training the laser on the particles. The method worked; the fat liquefied within minutes. Adah and Khalid filed a patent and formed a company, eLux Medical, to bring the procedure to the market. Though the company went out of business during the global pandemic of 2020, the basic procedure developed by the Almutairis is currently in use by many plastic surgeons. As of 2024 the worldwide market for liposuction as performed using nanoparticles stood at $272 million, and experts expected this figure to exceed $350 million within five years.

Today Almutairi continues to study nanotechnologies and carry out other scientific research at UCSD. As of 2024 she was a professor of pharmaceutical science with a joint appointment to the university's Jacobs School of Engineering. In addition, she remained the director of the Center for Excellence in Nanomedicine and Engineering. She has received multiple honors and awards for her work. That list includes a Takreem award, given by an Arab American organization to honor Middle East-

Mutlaq Almutairi

Adah Almutairi had no shortage of role models and mentors in her life. Perhaps the most influential, though, was her father, Mutlaq Almutairi. Mutlaq's father could not read or write and did not want his son to be educated. But even as a child, Mutlaq saw the value of learning. As a boy, he enrolled himself in school and got the education he wanted. He passed his love of learning down to his five children, all of whom became scientists, dentists, or physicians.

Mutlaq supported Adah in her desire to learn. She has spoken often of his confidence in her and the delight he took in her accomplishments—especially given that educating girls in Saudi Arabia remains controversial. However, together Adah and Mutlaq changed minds. "My father was very proud of me," Almutairi remarked in 2021. "When I became well known in the US . . . the people who were criticising him for sending his daughter away were the same people congratulating him." Mutlaq passed away in 2015 at age sixty-five, but he remains a great inspiration in his daughter's life and work.

Quoted in Tahira Yaqoob, "Woman of Substance: The Materials World of Adah Almutairi," *The National* (Abu Dhabi, UAE), August 27, 2021. www.thenationalnews.com.

ern Americans; Almutairi won the 2023 award in the category of Scientific and Technological Achievement. She has also been named one of the top ten influential female engineers in the world by *Forbes* magazine, and in 2023 she served as one of the jurors selecting the winners of the UNESCO Al Fozan prize awarded to young scientists around the globe. But nanoscience and its use in medicine remains closest to her heart. "Medicine is especially rewarding," she says. "I like to solve problems and have a positive impact on the world."[49]

Rashida Tlaib, US Representative

In addition to excelling in fields such as entertainment, medicine, and technology, Middle Eastern American women have made a name for themselves in government and politics. Mary Rose Oakar, elected to the US House of Representatives in 1977, held several important firsts where Congress was concerned. Descended from parents with roots in Syria and Lebanon, Oakar, as a representative from Ohio, was the first Arab American woman, first Lebanese American woman, and first Syrian American, male or female, to serve in either the House or Senate. Rosemary Barkett, the daughter of Syrian immigrant parents, became the first Arab American and the first woman to hold a seat on Florida's supreme court; she currently serves on an international court based in Netherlands. Other Middle Eastern women who have held high office in recent years include US representatives Stephanie Bice of Oklahoma, who is of Iranian descent; Anna Eshoo of California, who has Assyrian ancestors from what is now northern Iraq and southern Turkey; and Yassamin Ansari, an Iranian American elected to Congress from Arizona in 2024.

Perhaps the best-known Middle Eastern American woman in politics, though, is Rashida Tlaib. A Michigan native who was first elected to the US House of Representatives in 2018, Tlaib is the daughter of Palestinian immigrants. She is the first Palestinian American woman to serve in Congress, and one of the first two Muslim women to be elected to the House. Her years in Congress have been marked by her outspokenness. She is a fierce champion of many left-wing causes—such as advocating for universal health insurance, reproductive rights, and the rights of immigrants—and has been deeply critical of decisions made by both Republican and Democratic administrations. She is also a vocal opponent of Israel's policies toward Palestine and the Palestinian people, and she has worked to align American foreign policy with policies that would offer more support to Palestine. Tlaib relishes controversy and enjoys taking on powerful leaders on behalf of the people she represents. As she put it shortly after taking office, "I will never stop speaking truth to power."[50]

Rashida Tlaib was first elected to the US House of Representatives in 2018. She is the daughter of Palestinian immigrants and is the first Palestinian American woman to serve in Congress.

Early Life

Rashida Tlaib was born Rashida Harbi in Detroit, Michigan, in 1976. The oldest of fourteen children, she was often tasked with providing childcare to her younger siblings while she was growing up. She also was frequently needed to translate between Arabic and English for her mother, whose English skills were limited. Both experiences gave young Rashida opportunities to display responsibility and aid others in need. Living in a largely impoverished community within Detroit, a racially, ethnically, and religiously diverse city, also helped shape the person Rashida grew up to be. "All my experiences, my family background, and the culture I grew up in," Tlaib explained years later, "instilled in me the importance of taking care of the people who need it the most."[51]

In addition to becoming familiar with other people and their needs, Rashida focused on her own ambitions, particularly those in which education and family were concerned. After completing high school in 1994, Rashida graduated from Wayne State University with a major in political science four years later. That same year, she also married Fayez Tlaib. The couple, who have since divorced, have two sons, Adam and Yousif. Rashida Tlaib began her professional career immediately after college by taking a position at a social service agency in the Detroit area that primarily served Arab Americans.

> **"All my experiences, my family background, and the culture I grew up in instilled in me the importance of taking care of the people who need it the most."[51]**
>
> **—Rashida Tlaib**

The job was a good fit for her desire to help people, but Tlaib soon decided that she wanted to make a wider impact on the world. Accordingly, she enrolled at Thomas M. Cooley Law School in Lansing, Michigan, and earned her law degree in 2004. Having always been interested in politics, she chose to enter the world of state government and took a job as an intern with a Michigan state representative, a Democrat named Steve Tobocman. Tobocman appreciated and admired Tlaib's passion and skills and eventually hired her as a full-time member of his staff.

Donna Shalala

Donna Shalala is one of the most accomplished American politicians of Middle Eastern background. She not only served a term in the US House of Representatives but also worked in important positions in two presidential administrations. In addition, Shalala is an educator and has served on corporate boards for medical care and insurance companies.

Born in Cleveland, Ohio, in 1941, Shalala is of Lebanese descent. She studied political science and became a college professor in New York City. Much of her work has been in higher education. From 1980 to 1988 she served as president of New York's Hunter College and has held the presidency of two other universities as well.

Shalala is probably best known for her political involvement, though. In 1977 President Jimmy Carter appointed her as assistant secretary in the US Department of Housing and Urban Development. Later, she served as secretary of health and human services under President Bill Clinton from 1993 to 2001. And in 2018, the same year Rashida Tlaib won her seat in Congress, Shalala won a congressional seat from Florida. As of 2024 Shalala was the interim president at the New School in New York City.

Entering Politics

Because Michigan only allows a state representative to serve three terms, Tobocman was not eligible to run again for his seat in 2008. He urged Tlaib to enter the race, which she did. She ran a strong campaign in the Democratic primary, defeating seven other candidates to win the Democratic nomination. That November she captured Tobocman's seat in the general election with a huge majority in a heavily Democratic district. When she took office in early 2009, she became the first Muslim woman to hold a seat in the Michigan legislature and only the second to serve in any state legislature nationwide.

Tlaib threw herself into her work with enthusiasm. She focused on constituent services and advocated for the people of her district; she took on polluters, slumlords, and developers who ignored laws intended to safeguard ordinary citizens. Along the way Tlaib made several powerful enemies, one of whom launched an unsuccessful recall campaign against her. After three terms in the

Michigan House, Tlaib was term limited, just as Tobocman had been, and was no longer eligible to run again.

Hoping to remain in the legislature, Tlaib ran for the state senate in 2014. However, she narrowly lost a hard-fought primary to the incumbent. Since continuing in state government was no longer a possibility, Tlaib took a position at Sugar Law Center, a nonprofit organization that advocates for social justice, fighting corporate and governmental policies that threatens low-income workers and communities facing exploitation or environmental harms. During this time, her website explains, "Rashida took . . . to the courts, fighting racist emergency managers [and] abusive state agencies, and leading the fight for community benefits agreements that promote equitable development."[52]

US Representative

But Tlaib was eager to return to the life of an elected official. In 2017 she saw her chance. Late that year US representative John Conyers of Michigan resigned his position after a scandal involving sexual harassment. Tlaib ran in two primary elections in August 2018—one a special election to serve the remainder of Conyers's term in the House, and the other to fill the seat in a regular two-year term beginning the following January. Though Tlaib narrowly lost the primary for the special election, she defeated five opponents in the second primary and coasted to victory in November. She became the first Palestinian American woman elected to Congress.

Tlaib entered Congress during a time of great division among Americans. Republican Donald Trump had been elected president in 2016 despite having received fewer votes nationwide than his opponent, Democrat Hillary Clinton. While Trump's supporters backed him enthusiastically, his adversaries bitterly opposed him and his policies. Tlaib had been a longtime critic of the new president—in 2016 she had been made to leave a Trump rally in Michigan for heckling him—and she quickly became embroiled in controversy as she spoke out against Trump. She gained notoriety for her uncompromising rhetoric, such as her claim on her first day in the House that Trump should be impeached and removed from office. "President Donald Trump is a direct and serious threat to our country," she wrote a few days later, making her position clear. "The time for impeachment is now."[53]

> **"President Donald Trump is a direct and serious threat to our country. . . . The time for impeachment is now."[53]**
>
> **—Rashida Tlaib**

The House in 2019 included quite a few new members, many of them Democratic women. Tlaib joined forces with three of them—Ilhan Omar of Minnesota, Alexandria Ocasio-Cortez of New York, and Ayanna Pressley of Massachusetts—to form a group known as the Squad. All four were women of color, all were younger than the average representative, and all leaned considerably to the left even within the context of the relatively liberal Democratic Party. Each of these women wanted to change the way Congress worked. When California Democrat Nancy Pelosi ran for Speaker of the House—one of the most powerful positions in the federal government—the Squad threatened to oppose her. They

In 2019, Tlaib (far right) joined forces with other new members of congress, including Ayanna Pressley, Ilhan Omar, and Alexandria Ocasio-Cortez to form a group known as the Squad.

thought the seventy-eight-year-old Pelosi was too moderate and was out of touch with the needs of younger, poorer voters. "She doesn't speak about the issues that are important to the families of [my] district,"[54] Tlaib explained. In the end, all four members of the Squad voted for Pelosi, but Tlaib and the others had put the Democratic establishment on notice: they intended to be a force in the party going forward.

Controversy and Taking Stands

Upon taking office, Tlaib continued to work for policies that she had backed as a Michigan state legislator. She became known in Washington for her support for ordinary workers and the poor, for example, and she vehemently opposed legislation that she believed would unfairly benefit the rich. In the same vein, Tlaib has worked hard to establish limits on what auto insurance companies can charge consumers, and she has pushed for programs to provide affordable housing to middle- and lower-class buyers. "We need to talk about the working poor," she said upon taking office. "And [one] way we [help them] is access to homeownership. That is so key."[55] The environment, too, has remained a major concern of Tlaib's. In addition to advocating for reductions in air and water pollution, she has worked to raise awareness of climate change and its impact on the planet.

But as a part of the federal government, Tlaib has taken on other issues as well. A strong advocate for the rights of immigrants, she spoke out early on against the Trump administration's policies regarding migrants trying to enter the country through its southern border. The government's actions, which included the forced separation of families, appalled Tlaib. In late 2019 she visited the border and was horrified by what she saw. "I've been so deeply haunted by the image of a four-year-old boy," she reported after the trip, "[who] asked me in Spanish where his papa was."[56] Tlaib is one of several Democrats who has called for the abolition of the US Immigration and Customs Enforcement office, known as ICE. She advocates replacing it with what Tlaib and

Tlaib has been a fierce supporter of the Palestinians as the Israel-Hamas war leaves Gaza in ruins. She has charged that by supporting Israel, the United States is participating in genocide.

other members of the Squad called "an immigration system that reflects our values and respects the dignity and humanity of all."[57] Tlaib remained a critic of ICE under Democratic president Joe Biden as well.

Perhaps the most controversial stand Tlaib has taken, though, involves the Middle East. For many years there has been conflict, often violent, between the Jewish State of Israel and the largely Muslim Palestinian people who live in and around Israeli territory. Though US policy has tended to favor Israel, Tlaib has taken the side of the Palestinians. In 2019, after Tlaib and fellow Squad member Ilhan Omar supported a boycott of Israel, the Israeli government barred the two legislators from entering the country. Four years later, when Hamas—a terrorist organization based in Palestine—attacked Israel, the Israeli military responded with an ongoing show of force that as of late 2024 had led to the deaths of about forty-four thousand Palestinians. In a May 2024 statement, Tlaib called Israel an "apartheid state" in which Palestinians have few if any rights, and has charged that by supporting Israel, the United States is "actively participating in genocide."[58]

Goals and the Future

Some of Tlaib's goals have become reality. The House eventually impeached Trump twice during his first term, for example, though each time the Republican majority in the Senate rejected the charges and allowed him to stay in office. In other ways, she has had difficulty convincing more moderate Democrats to join her causes, let alone the members of the Republican Party. Nevertheless, Tlaib continues to speak her mind. "Rashida has a totally different political background from most people here," says Debbie Dingell, a fellow representative from Michigan. "She has the courage to jump over a fence to say what she is thinking."[59] Tlaib's outspokenness has made her a frequent target of Republican

Compassion and Vulnerability

Rashida Tlaib describes herself as an emotional person. In the House and on the campaign trail, Tlaib has cried in public on numerous occasions. Most often she cries when she is describing injustices, especially those committed against children and other people who are vulnerable to mistreatment. For example, she has frequently broken into tears when talking about undocumented immigrants and the plight of children at the border between Mexico and the United States.

Tlaib has been criticized for showing her feelings in general and for crying in particular. Some commentators and politicians, many but not all of them conservatives, have said that Tlaib's tears are inappropriate for a lawmaker. They argue that she should show less emotion and project instead an image of strength and calm.

Tlaib, however, rejects that advice. To her, crying is a perfectly acceptable response to tragedy and unjust behavior. Indeed, she sees tears as a positive, not a negative. As she puts it, "I [would] rather lead with compassion and show vulnerability. We stay connected to the people we serve when we allow ourselves to feel their pain."

Quoted in Jennifer Steinhauer, *The Firsts: The Inside Story of the Women Reshaping Congress*. Chapel Hill, NC: Algonquin, 2020, p. 135.

> “Rashida has a totally different political background from most people here. She has the courage to jump over a fence to say what she is thinking.”[59]
>
> —Debbie Dingell, US representative from Michigan

leaders, who have openly questioned her patriotism and her motives for supporting Palestine and the abolition of ICE. But the criticism has not fazed Tlaib. “I will outwork your hate,” she said to a heckler at a political rally in 2019. “I will outlove your hate.”[60]

Whatever her opponents elsewhere in the country may think of Tlaib, the voters of her district strongly approve of her. In both 2020 and 2022, Tlaib won the Democratic primary for her seat with about two-thirds of the vote, with only token opposition in the general election. In 2024, recognizing her popularity, no one challenged her in the party primary, and again she went on to an easy victory in November. Her seat appears safe for now, and despite the legislative setbacks she has experienced, Tlaib seems in no hurry to move on. If nothing else, she is deeply aware of the impact her job has on young Muslim women both in and out of her district. “I love when a Muslim father comes up to me and says to his daughter, ‘She is a Muslim,’” Tlaib told a journalist soon after taking office. “And I almost want to cry.”[61]

SOURCE NOTES

Introduction: Middle Eastern American Women

1. Quoted in Ray Hanania, "Lebanese-American Toni Breidinger Undaunted in Male-Dominated NASCAR Competition," *Arab News* (Riyadh, Saudi Arabia), June 24, 2023. www.arabnews.com.
2. Quoted in Sophie Brookover, "Inside Elyanna's World: How Creating 'Woledto' Allowed the Singer/Songwriter to Find a New Layer of Herself," Grammy Awards, April 11, 2024. www.grammy.com.
3. Rebecca Bengal, "Meet the Woman Leading the Fight to Protect the Arts in Trump's America," *Vogue*, April 10, 2017. www.vogue.com.

Chapter One: Mona Hanna, Pediatrician

4. Quoted in "Iraqi-American Doctor Who Blew the Whistle on Flint Water Crisis Asks, What If I Hadn't Been Here?," *New American Economy*, August 1, 2016. www.newamericaneconomy.org.
5. Quoted in Karen Bouffard, "Mona Hanna-Attisha: Resolve Exposed Flint Water Crisis," *Detroit (MI) News*, November 18, 2016. www.detroitnews.com.
6. Mona Hanna-Attisha, *What the Eyes Don't See*. New York: One World, 2018, p. 44.
7. Hanna-Attisha, *What the Eyes Don't See*, p. 19.
8. Hanna-Attisha, *What the Eyes Don't See*, p. 23.
9. Quoted in Ron Fonger, "Flint Water Problems: Switch Aimed to Save $5 Million—but at What Cost?," MLive, January 23, 2015. www.mlive.com.
10. Quoted in Anna Clark, "'Nothing to Worry About. The Water Is Fine': How Flint Poisoned Its People," *The Guardian* (Manchester, UK), July 3, 2018. www.theguardian.com.
11. Centers for Disease Control and Prevention, "Childhood Lead Poisoning Prevention," April 12, 2024. www.cdc.gov.
12. Quoted in Lindsey Smith, "Leaked Internal Memo Shows Federal Regulator's Concerns About Lead in Flint Water," *Michigan Public*, July 13, 2015. www.michiganpublic.org.
13. Quoted in Terry Gross, "Pediatrician Who Exposed Flint Water Crisis Shares Her 'Story of Resistance,'" *Fresh Air*, NPR, June 25, 2018. www.npr.org.
14. Hanna-Attisha, *What the Eyes Don't See*, p. 231.
15. Quoted in Gross, "Pediatrician Who Exposed Flint Water Crisis Shares Her 'Story of Resistance.'"
16. Quoted in Erin McCormick, "Michigan Doctor Who Revealed Flint Water Crisis Now Takes on Child Poverty," *The Guardian* (Manchester, UK), April 25, 2024. www.theguardian.com.
17. *Peerspectrum*, "28 Days That Saved a City," August 10, 2018. https://peerspectrum.com.

Chapter Two: Hoda Kotb, Broadcast Journalist

18. Quoted in H.W. Wilson, *Current Biography Yearbook 2011*. Hackensack, NJ: H.W. Wilson, 2011, p. 325.
19. Hoda Kotb with Jane Lorenzini, *Hoda*. New York: Simon & Schuster, 2010, p. 10.
20. Kotb, *Hoda*, p. 11.
21. Kotb, *Hoda*, p. 13.
22. Kotb, *Hoda*, p. 50.
23. Hoda Kotb with Jane Lorenzini, *Ten Years Later*. New York: Simon & Schuster, 2013, p. xi.
24. Quoted in H.W. Wilson, *Current Biography Yearbook 2011*, p. 326.
25. Kotb, *Hoda*, p. 105.
26. Kotb, *Hoda*, p. 193.
27. Quoted in Sarah Jacoby, "Hoda Kotb Reflects on Breast Cancer Diagnosis and Fertility: 'It Killed a Dream,'" *Today*, August 12, 2024. www.today.com.
28. Quoted in Rachel Paula Abrahamson et al., "Hoda's Kids: All About Hoda Kotb's Two Daughters, Hope and Haley," *Today*, September 26, 2024. www.today.com.
29. Quoted in Lindsay Lowe, "Hoda Kotb Opens Up About What She Plans to Do After Leaving *Today* and 'Instrumental' Guidance from Friends," *Today*, October 25, 2024. www.today.com.
30. Quoted in Stephanie Wenger, "Kathie Lee Gifford Praises 'Incredible' Hoda Kotb After She Announces *Today* Show Exit: 'Here's to New Adventures!,'" *People*, September 27, 2024. https://people.com.

Chapter Three: Rima Fakih, Miss USA

31. Quoted in Hussein Yassine, "Rima Fakih & Sal's Campaign for Lebanon Raised $1.2 Million So Far," The 961, August 28, 2020. www.the961.com.
32. Quoted in Associated Press, "Miss USA from Powerful Shiite Family," NBC News, May 17, 2010. www.nbcnews.com.
33. Quoted in vtsang, "Rima Fakih Slaiby: Driven by Love and Empowering Uniqueness," *Harper's Bazaar*, October 31, 2022. https://bazaarvietnam.vn.
34. World Lebanese Cultural Union, "Miss Lebanon Emigrant," March 21, 2008. https://web.archive.org.
35. Quoted in Jodi Rempala, "Miss USA Rima Fakih: Living a Dream," *Press & Guide*, May 24, 2010. www.pressandguide.com.
36. Quoted in Rempala, "Miss USA Rima Fakih."
37. Quoted in Associated Press, "Miss USA from Powerful Shiite Family."
38. Quoted in Christian Women in Media Association, "Rima Fakih, First Muslim Miss USA Winner, Converts to Christianity," CWIMA, May 17, 2016. https://cwima.org.
39. Quoted in Dan Gilgoff, "Crash Course in Islam from Miss USA," *Belief Blog*, CNN, May 21, 2010. https://web.archive.org.
40. Quoted in Jasmine Viel, "Skid Row's School on Wheels Hoping to Help Homeless Students Get off the Streets," CBS News, August 22, 2022. www.cbsnews.com.
41. Quoted in IMDb, "Rima Fakih: Biography." www.imdb.com.

Chapter Four: Adah Almutairi, Nanoscientist

42. Quoted in Tahira Yaqoob, "Woman of Substance: The Materials World of Adah Almutairi," *The National* (Abu Dhabi, UAE), August 27, 2021. www.thenationalnews.com.
43. Quoted in Yaqoob, "Woman of Substance."
44. Quoted in Yaqoob, "Woman of Substance."
45. Quoted in Benefunder, "The Art of Falling Apart." www.benefunder.com.
46. Quoted in Heather Buschman, "Adah Almutairi Breaks Down Barriers at Berlin's 'Falling Walls' Conference," *UC San Diego Today*, January 8, 2015. https://today.ucsd.edu.
47. Quoted in Buschman, "Adah Almutairi Breaks Down Barriers at Berlin's 'Falling Walls' Conference."
48. Quoted in Lauren K. Wolf, "Liposuction Goes Nano," *Chemical & Engineering News*, June 16, 2014. https://cen.acs.org.
49. Quoted in Yaqoob, "Woman of Substance."

Chapter Five: Rashida Tlaib, US Representative

50. Quoted in Niraj Warikoo, "Rep. Rashida Tlaib: Migrants 'Treated like Cattle' in Detention Centers," *Detroit (MI) Free Press*, July 8, 2019. https://tlaib.house.gov.
51. Quoted in Cooley Law School, "Trailblazing Tlaib Elected to Historic Role," *Benchmark Column*, July 2010. https://issuu.com.
52. Congresswoman Rashida Tlaib, "About Congresswoman Rashida Tlaib." https://tlaib.house.gov.
53. Quoted in Mark Osborne, "New Congresswoman Rashida Tlaib Not Apologizing for Cursing Out Trump in Call for Impeachment," ABC News, January 4, 2019. https://abcnews.go.com.
54. Quoted in Felicia Sonmez, "Rashida Tlaib Says She's 'Probably Not' Going to Back Pelosi for Democratic Leader," *Washington Post*, August 9, 2018. www.washingtonpost.com.
55. Quoted in *Detroit Free Press* Editorial Staff, "Rashida Tlaib: Matty Moroun Prepared Me for Donald Trump," *Detroit (MI) Free Press*, September 22, 2019. www.freep.com.
56. Quoted in Jennifer Steinhauer, *The Firsts: The Inside Story of the Women Reshaping Congress*. Chapel Hill, NC: Algonquin, 2020, p. 126.
57. Congresswoman Rashida Tlaib, "Progressive Congresswomen Slam ICE and CBP: Not One More Dollar," June 22, 2019. https://tlaib.house.gov.
58. Congresswoman Rashida Tlaib, "Tlaib Statement on the Ongoing Genocide of Palestinians and Invasion of Rafah," May 7, 2024. https://tlaib.house.gov.
59. Quoted in Steinhauer, *The Firsts*, p. 76.
60. Quoted in Steinhauer, *The Firsts*, p. 153.
61. Quoted in Steinhauer, *The Firsts*, p. 197.

FOR FURTHER RESEARCH

Books

Mona Hanna-Attisha, *What the Eyes Don't See*. New York: One World, 2018.

Hoda Kotb with Jane Lorenzini, *Hoda*. New York: Simon & Schuster, 2010.

Ferial Masry and Susan Chenard, *Running for All the Right Reasons: A Saudi-Born Woman's Pursuit of Democracy*. Syracuse, NY: Syracuse University Press, 2008.

Michael W. Suleiman et al., eds., *Arab American Women: Representation and Refusal*. Syracuse, NY: Syracuse University Press, 2021.

Internet Sources

Albani Berryhill, "Celebrate These Notable Women for Arab American Heritage Month," *Blog & News*, Women's Foundation of Colorado, April 27, 2023. https://blog.wfco.org.

Karen Bouffard, "Mona Hanna-Attisha: Resolve Exposed Flint Water Crisis," *Detroit (MI) News*, November 18, 2016. www.detroitnews.com.

Heather Buschman, "Adah Almutairi Breaks Down Barriers at Berlin's 'Falling Walls' Conference," *UC San Diego Today*, January 8, 2015. https://today.ucsd.edu.

Anna Clark, "'Nothing to Worry About. The Water Is Fine': How Flint Poisoned Its People," *The Guardian* (Manchester, UK), July 3, 2018. www.theguardian.com.

Nisreen Eadeh, "Honoring 30 Influential Arab American Women for International Women's Day," Arab America, March 8, 2017. www.arabamerica.com.

Gail Hafif, "6 Arab American Women You Should Know About," She Should Run, August 17, 2021. https://sheshouldrun.org.

Sarah Jacoby, "Hoda Kotb Reflects on Breast Cancer Diagnosis and Fertility: 'It Killed a Dream,'" *Today*, August 12, 2024. www.today.com.

Jodi Rempala, "Miss USA Rima Fakih: Living a Dream," *Press & Guide*, May 24, 2010. www.pressandguide.com.

Jessica Weingartner, "Honoring Arab American Heritage, Stories, and Changemakers," Facing History and Ourselves, April 12, 2024. www.facinghistory.org.

Tahira Yaqoob, "Woman of Substance: The Materials World of Adah Almutairi," *The National* (Abu Dhabi, UAE), August 27, 2021. www.thenationalnews.com.

Websites

Arab American Women's Business Council

https://aawbc.org

This organization is based in Dearborn, Michigan. It assists Middle Eastern American women in business by offering guidance in starting their own companies. It also provides mentorship and networking opportunities along with scholarships.

Congresswoman Rashida Tlaib

https://tlaib.house.gov

This is the official website of US representative Rashida Tlaib. In addition to offering information about important government issues of the day and Tlaib's positions on them, it includes biographical details about Tlaib and an assortment of news items.

National Arab American Women's Association

https://naawa.org

This is an organization of Middle Eastern American women. It offers community support for Arab American women, along with advocating for social justice concerns. The website also provides educational information about issues faced by women in the Arab American community.

Smithsonian American Women's History Museum

https://womenshistory.si.edu

The museum's goal is to expand the story of America through often-untold accounts and accomplishments of women. Pages for middle school and high school students present the stories of women in various fields and from all different backgrounds.

INDEX

Note: Boldface page numbers indicate illustrations.

PICTURE CREDITS

Cover: Kathy Hutchins/Shutterstock

5: Bruce Alan Bennett/Shutterstock
8: Adam Stoltman/Alamy Stock Photo
11: Atomazul/Shutterstock
14: Associated Press
18: MediaPunch Inc/Alamy Stock Photo
23: a katz/Shutterstock
25: Debby Wong/Shutterstock
28: WENN Rights Ltd/Alamy Stock Photo
32: WENN Rights Ltd/Alamy Stock Photo
35: Image Press Agency/Sipa USA/Newscom
38: Love Employee/Shutterstock
42: bluestork/Shutterstock
47: Phil Pasquini/Shutterstock
51: MIKE THIELER/UPI/Newscom
53: Maxim Elramsisy/Shutterstock

ABOUT THE AUTHOR

Stephen Currie has written dozens of books for young adults, including *Digital Literacy: What Is It and Why Does It Matter?* and *Black Immigrants* for ReferencePoint Press. He has also taught grade levels ranging from kindergarten to college. He lives in the Hudson Valley of New York.